New Vanguard • 63

Fighting Ships of the Far East (2)

Japan and Korea AD 612–1639

Stephen Turnbull • Illustrated by Wayne Reynolds

First published in Great Britain in 2003 by Osprey Publishing,
Midland House, West Way, Botley, Oxford OX2 0PH, UK
44-02 23rd St, Suite 219, Long Island City, NY 11101, USA
E-mail: info@ospreypublishing.com

Transferred to digital print on demand 2009

First published 2003
1st impression 2003

Printed and bound by PrintOnDemand-Worldwide.com, Peterborough, UK

A CIP catalogue record for this book is available from the British Library

ISBN: 978 1 84176 470 8

Editorial by Simone Drinkwater
Design by Melissa Orrom Swan
Index by Alison Worthington
Originated by The Electronic Page Company, Cwmbran, UK

Author's Dedication
To Gill Randall

Artist's Note
Readers may care to note that the original paintings from which the colour plates in this book were prepared are available for private
sale. All reproduction copyright whatsoever is retained by the Publishers. All enquiries should be addressed to:
Wayne Reynolds
5 Kirkstall Mount
Kirkstall
Leeds
West Yorkshire
LS5 3DT
UK
The Publishers regret that they can enter into no correpondence upon this matter.

Editor's Note
All images are credited to the author unless otherwise noted.

FOR A CATALOGUE OF ALL BOOKS PUBLISHED BY OSPREY
MILITARY AND AVIATION PLEASE CONTACT:

Osprey Direct, c/o Random House Distribution Center,
400 Hahn Road, Westminster, MD 21157
Email: uscustomerservice@ospreypublishing.com

Osprey Direct, The Book Service Ltd, Distribution Centre,
Colchester Road, Frating Green, Colchester, Essex, CO7 7DW
E-mail: customerservice@ospreypublishing.com

www.ospreypublishing.com

FIGHTING SHIPS OF THE FAR EAST (2) JAPAN AND KOREA AD 612–1639

INTRODUCTION

My previous volume covering fighting ships of the Far East dealt with China and Southeast Asia from the Han to the early Ming dynasties. Here the attention will be given to Korea and Japan from the times of the wars between the Three Kingdoms of Korea, in which Japan took part, to the Seclusion Edict in Japan, which effectively drew Japanese maritime enterprise to a close. The Ming dynasty of China will also come into the story, as will Siam (Thailand), which made its own unique contribution to the history of Japanese naval warfare.

Over the centuries, naval relations between Korea and Japan appear to have alternated between peaceful trade and outright hostility, but this impression can be highly misleading, as much of what passes for ordinary mercantile activity turns out to be conducted by the Japanese pirate fleets that pillaged the coasts of Korea and China in a long lasting tradition that culminated in the greatest pirate raid of all: Hideyoshi's invasion of Korea in 1592. This was the conflict that involved Ming China

The Korean navy, from a painted screen of the 18th century, when the craze for building turtle ships was at its height.

and almost dragged in Siam, but resulted in Korea developing East Asia's most famous war vessel: the legendary turtle ship, which is described in full technical detail for the first time in this book.

In my previous books in the New Vanguard Series, *Siege Weapons of the Far East* Volumes 1 and 2, it was noted how in the field of Far Eastern siege warfare Japan was very much the odd man out. In continental East Asia siege crossbows and traction trebuchets were used for the primary purpose of battering down the walls of fortified towns, but in Japan, with no tradition of walled cities but with plenty of mountain-top castles made of wood, siege machines were primarily either incendiary weapons using fire arrows, or anti-personnel devices. When we turn to naval warfare we see a similar distinction between continental and Japanese practice. As Volume 1 of the present work showed, the Chinese preference in naval fighting was for bombardment from a distance, helped on occasions by the use of 'striking arms'; the curious 'anti-grappling irons' that held off an enemy at a convenient range. Such techniques reached their culmination in the Korean turtle ship, while Japan, by contrast, preferred to conduct naval warfare by grappling and boarding, a priority shared elsewhere only in the very different situation of the Southeast Asian river war barge.

Many organisations and individuals have been more than helpful in the preparation of this volume, but I would particularly like to thank the Royal Armouries Museum, Leeds; the National Maritime Museum; the War Memorial, Seoul; the staff of the turtle ship displays and museums at Yosu, Tongyong and Noryang; the National Museum of Thailand and the Museum of Chinese History in Beijing.

Typical Japanese warships in action at the battle of Yashima in 1184. We see the giant Taira Noto no kami Noritsune hurling Minamoto samurai into the water.

FIGHTING SHIPS AND NAVAL WARFARE IN JAPAN AND KOREA

Early naval expeditions between Japan and Korea

The naval traditions of Japan and Korea were closely linked for much of their written history. There was first a very close geographical relationship: whereas the Japanese island of Tsushima is 120 miles from the Japanese mainland, it is only 30 miles from Korea, and as the island of Iki lies conveniently between Tsushima and Japan, navigation and trade has always been a comparatively straightforward operation. Yet this has also meant that the sea route across the Korean Strait was the classic invasion route in both directions. This was the path taken by the Mongol invasions of Japan in 1274 and 1281, and the Japanese invasions of Korea in 1592 and 1597. Most controversially of all, it was across the Korea Strait that another invasion had passed during the first centuries of the Christian era. In Korean tradition, this was the arrival of a Korean princess in Japan who founded the Japanese imperial line. In Japanese tradition the situation is reversed, and the occasion was the invasion of Korea by the Empress Jingu, who carried in her womb the future emperor who was to be deified as Hachiman the god of war.

Both countries, however, agree that sizeable Japanese expeditionary forces crossed over to Korea on several occasions to assist Paekche, one of the three early Korean kingdoms, against its rivals Koguryo and Silla. Tang-dynasty China also became involved, although very little naval fighting is recorded on any occasion. The 170 Japanese ships recorded in the spring of 662 were probably no more than troop carriers, although there was some naval action in the battle of the Paekch'on River in 663. Japan moved on to the defensive after 666 when Tang China defeated Koguryo. An invasion of Japan by Silla was daily expected, and in 894 there was a naval battle between Japanese and Korean ships during which crossbows were used.

Admiral Yi Sun-sin, the great hero of Korea, shown in this portrait in the shrine to him at Noryang.

5

For the clearest accounts of Japanese naval warfare we have to wait until the Gempei War of 1180–85, when rival samurai armies fought at sea using tactics similar to those they would have used on land, with ships being reduced to the role of artificial floating battlefields. For example, in 1183 there was a strange sea battle where the ships were tied together and planking laid across them to make a platform for fighting, but accounts of 'real' naval fighting are so rare that it is strange to note that Dan no Ura, the conflict which ended the Gempei Wars in 1185, was one of the most decisive sea battles in history.

The Mongol invasions of Japan

The 13th century was a time of comparative peace for Japan, broken only by minor rebellions and by Korea's unwilling participation in the major naval operations that were the Mongol attempts at an invasion of Japan. Khubilai Khan, who had conquered Korea, issued an order for the Koreans to build 900 ships. The invasion journey from Pusan took two weeks, during which the Mongol force ravaged Tsushima and Iki, and made landfall in the sheltered Hakata Bay, where the modern city of Fukuoka now stands. There was some savage fighting, but the Mongols withdrew after two days.

For the next few years the Japanese were in a state of alert. One measure, never actually carried out, was a planned seaborne raid by Japan on Korea to be led by the Kyushu general Shoni Tsunesuke. That same year (1276) the construction began of a defensive wall around Hakata Bay. The Mongol preparations for the 1281 invasion were on a much larger scale than those of 1274, and it is clear from the fact that farming implements were included on board the ships that the Mongols intended a permanent occupation of Japan. Six hundred warships were ordered from southern China, in addition to 900 from Korea. The Mongols established themselves on two islands in the bay, one of which, Shiga, was connected to the mainland by a narrow spit of land. From these islands they launched attacks against the Japanese for about a week, to which the Japanese responded with night raids against the Mongol ships.

One of the stone anchors used by the Mongol invasion fleet recovered from the sea off Hakata. (Richard Turnbull)

The Mongols were eventually destroyed not by samurai but by the weather in the form of the famous *kami kaze*, the wind of the gods. Forced by the Japanese raids to stay in their ships, and unable to drop anchor in protected harbour waters, the Mongol fleet was obliterated. But in spite of this great victory the perceived threat from Yuan China continued for many years, and in 1301 it was believed that a Chinese invasion fleet had been seen off the coast of

A sketch showing how the stone anchor was mounted in a wooden frame.

The Korean navy hits back at the Japanese wako (pirates) by raiding the pirate base on Tsushima Island in 1389.

Satsuma Province. The samurai of the Hakata area who provided coastal defences were taken off alert only in 1312, but by this time other Japanese had already hit back in a way that was to add another chapter to the history of Japanese and Korean naval warfare.

The curse of the wako

From the time of the Mongol invasions onwards nearly all the instances of naval conflict between Japan and Korea involved Japanese pirates. The Koreans called them *waegu*, which was rendered into Japanese as *wako*, the 'brigands from the country of Wa', but this was just the most polite expression for these brutal ruffians. Centuries earlier they had attacked only Japanese targets, but they extended their horizons to Korea during the 1220s. In 1227 some exemplary beheadings, witnessed by a specially invited Korean dignitary, proclaimed the official Japanese government line with profound clarity.

In the 14th century, however, the wako started up again, and between 1376 and 1385 there were 174 recorded wako raids on Korea. Some of these expeditions amounted to short-term invasions of Korea, with as many as 3,000 wako penetrating far from the coast, ravaging Kaesong, the Koryo capital, and taking slaves from as far north as P'yongyang. Some wako bands even attacked the Chinese coast, but the first Ming emperor, who had been the victor of the epic naval battle of Poyang Lake in 1363 and was no stranger to sea power, threatened to invade Japan if the wako were not controlled.

Meanwhile the Koreans took direct action. In 1380 over 500 Japanese pirate ships were set ablaze at the mouth of the Kum River, and in 1383 Admiral Chong Chi used cannon fire to chase away more than 100 Japanese ships. The Koreans went on to attack pirate bases on Tsushima in 1389 and 1419. In that same year a Japanese pirate fleet of 30 ships set sail for China from Tsushima, not knowing that the Ming were shadowing their every move. They were ambushed off the Liaodong peninsula and as many as 1,500 wako were relieved of their heads. There was little heard of the wako in Chinese waters for many years to come.

Details of a typical seki bune's bows are given in this print of the samurai Goto Mototsugu.

Towards the end of the 15th century commercial relations between Japan and Korea moved on from piracy to the establishment of three licensed Japanese trading enclaves on the southern Korean coast. But so economically aggressive were the Japanese merchants that Korea tried to expel them, and in 1510 a major riot developed, to which the *daimyo* (feudal lords) of Tsushima, the So family, responded by attacking Koje island in an echo of the wako raids of old. Pirates also raided vast areas of China, with 467 incidents being recorded between 1551 and 1560. Wako was still the name used for the brigands, but the majority of them were no longer Japanese but a mixed bag of Chinese renegades, Portuguese freebooters and Japanese mercenaries in one big happy family. One of them, the Chinese pirate Wang Zhi, who was beheaded in 1551, had the audacity to make his headquarters on the Japanese island of Hirado.

From pirates to sea lords

By the mid-16th century there was also considerable warlike activity going on in Japanese waters. Following the Onin War in 1467 the centralised authority of the Shogun had virtually collapsed, and just as the more landlubberly daimyo had established their territories by the thoroughly respectable business of stealing one another's land and building castles on it, so the more astute seafarers of Kyushu and the Inland Sea entered the new Japanese aristocracy through the means of naval warfare.

In at least one case there was an intermediate stage between pirate and daimyo which consisted of the 'sea lord', for want of a better term, selling his services to larger fry. Murakami Takeyoshi (1533–1604) had long ruled the roost from his castle located on the island of Noshima in Iyo Province, one of the busiest and narrowest straits of Japan's Inland

In this remarkable illustration from Ehon Taikoki a Japanese kobaya, to which extra protection has been added in the form of bamboo screens, goes into action against a fleet of very fanciful Korean turtle ships, expressive of the artist's flight of fancy.

Sea. 'The people of the shores and sea coasts of other provinces each year pay him tribute for fear of being destroyed,' wrote one chronicler, and when war broke about between Oda Nobunaga and the Mori family both sides courted his services.

Experienced sea dogs such as Murakami provided a vital contribution to samurai warfare during this century which became known as the Sengoku (Warring States) Period, and it was only the most completely landlocked of the Japanese daimyo who felt that they could dispense with a navy. The Hojo, who had direct access to the Pacific Ocean, are known to have fought naval battles against the Satomi family, and even Takeda Shingen, whose lands encompassed the central mountain region of Japan, and who fought the Uesugi on one side and the Hojo on the other to gain access to the sea, maintained his own inland navy on Lake Suwa.

In 1569, when the Takeda lands included former Imagawa territories on the Pacific coast, five ships became the core of a new Takeda navy under the former Imagawa retainer Tsuchiya Sadatsuna. The fleet grew quickly in response to the threat from the neighbouring Hojo, and by 1575, when Tsuchiya Sadatsuna was killed at Nagashino, there were 50 *ataka bune*-type ships in the Takeda navy. They went into action against the Hojo in 1580 near Omosu in Izu Province. Takeda Katsuyori had set up his headquarters on land, from where he could watch his admirals Mukai Masashige and his son Masakatsu launch an attack on the Hojo ships, which outnumbered them three to one. There was some fierce fighting before the ships disengaged, but even this demonstration of another dimension to the Takeda fighting capacity was not sufficient to save them from their ultimate collapse in 1582.

From 1560 the most powerful daimyo in Japan was Oda Nobunaga, who defeated a series of rivals to control central Japan. The Mori, whose territories lay to the west, came into direct conflict with him when they began supporting his deadliest enemies, the Buddhist fanatics of the Ikko-ikki, whose head-quarters were the fortified cathedrals of Nagashima and Ishiyama Honganji, the latter being located where Osaka castle now stands. This gave the Ikko-ikki a direct outlet to the Inland Sea, and Mori obligingly kept them supplied by this route. The result was the first battle of Kizugawaguchi in 1578, which is described in a later section. There were few other naval battles during the Sengoku Period. The invasions of Shikoku and Kyushu by Hideyoshi saw ships being used only for transport purposes, but the siege of the Hojo castle of Shimoda in 1590 provides a unique example of a siege being conducted largely from the sea by certain of Hideyoshi's generals who would soon have a wider maritime remit during the invasions of Korea.

An excellent depiction of the mon on the sails of daimyos' ships.

The Japanese invasions of Korea

The days of the genuine Japanese wako came abruptly to an end in 1587, when the dictator Toyotomi Hideyoshi supplemented his famous Sword Hunt, which disarmed the peasantry, with a lesser-known edict curtailing piracy. This would have been very good news for Korea had it not been for the fact that in less than five years' time these former pirates would be taking part in an official invasion of Korea, which to the average Korean was no more and no less than the worst wako raid in history.

The Korean War is of vital importance in this work because the widespread naval fighting that took place involved all three countries of Japan, China and Korea. At one point it also threatened to suck in other

Toyotomi Hideyoshi watches as his invasion fleet departs for Korea in this detail from Ehon Taikoki.

nations, because King Naresuan of Siam offered to assist China by deploying the Siamese fleet against Japan. This was no empty gesture, but by the time the Ming rejected his kind offer in February 1593 the first Japanese invasion was already heading for defeat. The naval campaigns under the celebrated Korean Admiral Yi Sun-sin were among the most important events of the conflict, and, along with land-based Ming intervention and guerrilla warfare, finally tipped the balance against Japan.

It is a notable feature of the Japanese invasion that almost no planning went into the naval side of the operation. To Hideyoshi the fleet he impressed from the daimyo of western Japan was simply there to provide transport. The ships had no protection other than that provided by the samurai who sailed on them during the short journey from Tsushima to Pusan. The thought that the Korean navy might attack them never seems to have entered anyone's mind, yet we do know that Hideyoshi had tried to obtain two Portuguese ships for use in the operation, a request that was politely declined. However, the experience of the unopposed crossing only served to confirm this optimism, and it was several weeks after the Japanese landed before the first Korean ship went into action against them. One reason for this was that Pusan lay within the sea area covered by Admiral Yi's incompetent colleagues, both of whom fled as soon as the Japanese armada was spotted. For an entire night the whole Japanese fleet lay crammed together in Pusan harbour, and nothing, not even one fireship, came by to disturb them. Yi was only able to join in the resistance long after the Japanese army had established its bridgehead, and what naval activity took place was confined to the depredations of maritime foraging parties who ransacked the southern coast of Korea, much as the wako of old.

When the Japanese withdrew in 1593, leaving a line of coastal fortresses for the occupying forces, Yi kept up the pressure on them from the sea, harassing naval supply columns and fighting the occasional skirmish. But when the Japanese returned in 1597 Yi had been removed from his post, and the Japanese won their only naval victory of the campaign against the unreliable Won Kyun. This led to Yi's reinstatement and a major naval victory at Myongyang. The entry of Ming China into the war added a new fleet to Korea's maritime capability, but the battle of Sunch'on, which combined land and sea warfare, was a disaster for the Chinese navy. At Noryang in 1598 the Japanese suffered their last naval defeat as they attempted to escape for home, but Admiral Yi was shot when the battle was at its height and died, like Lord Nelson, aboard his flagship.

Seapower and the Tokugawa

There was almost no naval warfare involved in the decisive Sekigahara campaign of 1600 that won the shogunate for Tokugawa Ieyasu, but ships were to play their part in the final showdown with the Toyotomi at the siege of Osaka. Osaka castle was surrounded by extensive waterways, and the Tokugawa exploited this to the full, bombarding Toyotomi outposts from on board ship, and fighting one amphibious operation at Kizugawa and one naval battle at Toda-Fukushima.

The Tokugawa shogunate, who proceeded to rule Japan for two and a half centuries after Sekigahara, are not commonly remembered for their maritime entrepreneurship, but it was only in the years after the Seclusion Edict of 1639 that Japan turned its back on naval activity. In the early years of Tokugawa Ieyasu's reign Japanese maritime enterprise had actually increased. Unfortunately, piracy had again reared its ugly head, but now the inhabitants of Siam, Cambodia and Vietnam were the chosen victims rather than the Koreans or the Chinese. In December 1605 a certain John Davis became the first Englishman ever to be killed by a Japanese when his ship was involved in a fight with Japanese pirates off the Siamese coast, and in 1614 men of the East India Company killed eight Japanese in a skirmish at Ayuthia, the Siamese capital.

The new generation of wako were clearly operating against the wishes of the Japanese government, because when the king of Cambodia wrote to complain to Tokugawa Ieyasu, the shogun replied that the king had his full permission to punish them according to his country's own laws.

The ship in which Yamada Nagamasa sailed to Siam (Thailand), drawn from a votive picture in his family temple in Shizuoka. Yamada Nagamasa (1578–1633), whose life has been greatly embellished by legend, was born in Suruga Province, and claimed to be a grandson of Oda Nobunaga. In 1615, when the political crisis of the Osaka campaign made thoughts of foreign adventure a risky business, he sailed from Osaka in secret in a vessel bound for Formosa (Taiwan). After some time there, he sailed for Siam.

In 1623 the king of Siam wrote to the second shogun, Tokugawa Hidetada, whose reply, delivered in a suitably haughty samurai tone, was exactly what the king wished to read. These so-called 'merchants' were expendable, and the Siamese government should not hesitate in exterminating them, because 'merchants are fond of gain and given up to greed, and abominable fellows of this kind ought not to escape punishment'.

The most famous samurai ever to sail abroad in this shadowy era that blended merchant with mercenary and marauder was Yamada Nagamasa (1578–1633), whose life has been greatly embellished by legend. He was born in Suruga Province, and claimed to be a grandson of Oda Nobunaga. In 1615, when the political crisis of the Osaka campaign made thoughts of foreign adventure a risky business, he sailed secretly from Osaka in a vessel bound for Formosa (Taiwan). After some time there he sailed for Siam, where he set up in business, but his military skills proved to be more useful to his hosts, and he soon found himself fighting for the king of Siam. He was so successful that he rose to become the king's right-hand man, but the royal confidence he enjoyed inevitably led to jealousy and accusations of power politics. When the old king became ill in 1633 a minister arranged for Yamada Nagamasa to be poisoned.

The Shimabara Rebellion of 1638 was the last samurai civil war, but there was little naval involvement other than a token bombardment of the anti-Tokugawa rebels by a Dutch ship. The Manchu invasions of Korea also involved very little naval activity, so by the time both nations were to take to the seas again warships were very different vessels indeed.

A Korean ship of the Koryo Period in the War Memorial Museum, Seoul. A treatise of 1009 records 75 warships in the Koryo navy. All were of comparatively simple construction, but were known for being very strong.

TECHNIQUES AND TYPES OF KOREAN SHIPS AND SHIPBUILDING

The Korean shipbuilding tradition

As with the classic Chinese junk described in Volume 1, there was a tremendous amount of tradition involved in Korean shipbuilding techniques. The favourite wood for shipbuilding was always pine, with oak being employed for pegs. The wood was usually allowed to season incompletely so that it would bend easily and not become too stiff. Bending was done using a combination of a fire being burned below the plank and water being poured on above.

The bottom of the ship was first laid down, and then the side planks were built up. Wherever possible each plank extended from bow to stern. To draw the planks together prior to being pegged, a rope was fastened under the lower and over the upper planks and then drawn tight by tension exerted through a lever inserted under the rope. The pegs were driven diagonally down from the outside of the upper plank and projected on the inside of the lower plank. These ends were later sawn off and the outer ends countersunk. It was often the case that each plank was stepped out a little so that Korean vessels had the appearance of being clinker-built. The ship now resembled a box or trough without the ends. Very heavy planks or rounded beams were now placed across it to hold the boat together, and features such as decking and supports for the mast were added.

The Korean oar was virtually identical to the Chinese *yuloh*, which operated on the principle of a screw, and consisted of a broad blade of hardwood joined to a central section and a handle. The yuloh rested on a fulcrum at about its point of balance. A rope was fastened at one end to the handle, and at the other end to a ring bolt on the deck to balance the weight of the blade and keep it at the correct angle as it was moved. A pull on the rope also controlled the feathering of the blade.

The crew on one side of the full-sized reproduction turtle ship at Yosu.

Early Korean fighting ships

A vessel-shaped container preserved in the National Museum of Korea provides the earliest evidence of what a Korean ship looked like. It dates from the Three Kingdoms Period, and resembles a canoe with a sharp prow and is wide amidships. It is propelled by one steersman with a yuloh-type oar, and there are no indications that it has any military function. That larger sea-going vessels already existed by then is confirmed by records of embassies travelling to China by sea as early as AD 32. Paekche sent envoys in 373, as did Silla in 380, using vessels called *kyontangson* (China-bound ships), which were double-masted sailing vessels resembling Chinese junks, each carrying 150 passengers.

Fighting ships of the Koryo dynasty

Details of Korean ships during the wars between the Three Kingdoms are as sparse as the sources for the Japanese equivalents, but true military vessels developed rapidly during the Koryo dynasty (935–1392) because of the need to defend Korea against Japanese and Jurchen pirates. By the beginning of the 11th century Koryo shipbuilders had produced the kwason (spear vessel), a ship built specifically for ramming Jurchen vessels, but this was just one type of warship among others. The largest carried a crew of between 100 and 200 sailors, and one was said to be so large that it was possible to race a horse round the deck!

A treatise of 1009 records 75 warships in the Koryo navy, and in 1123 a visiting Song official described a Koryo ship in the words, 'The structure of the vessel and the oars was especially simple, with a single mast standing in the middle of the ship; there was no forecastle, and there was a steering oar. I saw ten such vessels.' This description matches the design of a ship engraved on the back of a bronze mirror of the Koryo dynasty preserved in Seoul. The Song official also noted larger 'official vessels' with a cabin with doors and portholes and two masts. There would therefore appear to be two main types of ship in Koryo service: one derived from Song Chinese styles, the other a native Korean version, of which strength and simplicity appear to have been the main characteristics. That Koryo ships were much stronger than contemporary Chinese vessels is shown by the fact that whereas nearly all the Yuan ships that took part in the Mongol invasion of Japan in 1281 were destroyed by the kami kaze, little damage was suffered by some 900 Korean ships that accompanied them.

Choson-dynasty warships

Shipbuilding during the Choson dynasty was distinguished by its emphasis on warships. Three types were identified: the *tae maengson* (big warship), the *chung maengson* (medium warship) and the *so maengson* (small warship), carrying crews of 80, 60 and 30 sailors respectively. In addition there were reserve and support vessels called *mugun* (literally 'non-combatant'). The designs continued to emphasise solidity and strength rather than speed, and the ships were notable for their width, but the equivalent ships built exclusively for river work were comparatively longer and narrower. Surviving illustrations confirm the very simple, box-like appearance of the ordinary Korean warship.

With the appointment of a certain Sin Suk-chu to the post of director of the Office of Shipbuilding in 1465, new priorities were given to military ships, and a

The war drum is beaten on the full-sized reproduction turtle ship at Yosu while an archer looses an arrow through the arrow slit.

further decision was made to build troop-carrying vessels. Three types were built, all called *p'yongjoson*, which could easily be converted to peacetime cargo-carrying use by removing the upper structures. In February 1550 Korea's first paddle-wheel ship was laid down. It was based on written Chinese descriptions and seems to have resembled the Song dynasty's 23-wheel version illustrated in Volume 1 of this work. It was, however, only used for commercial purposes.

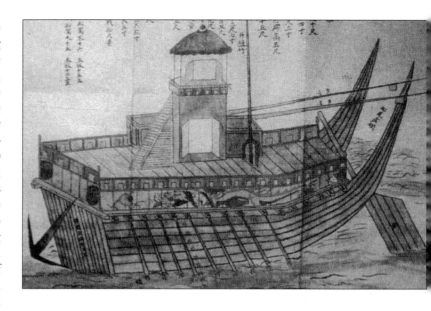

A p'anokson, the standard fighting ship that was the backbone of the Korean navy during the war against Japan. It has a deck castle and two decks, one for oarsmen and the other for fighting. Note the dragon painted on the side. P'anokson always outnumbered the better-known turtle ships.

In 1413 an updated version of the old *kwason* (spear vessel) was developed and given the name of the *kobukson* (turtle ship). This is the first appearance of this name in Korean history, but the 15th-century version bore little resemblance to the famous battleships of 1592. Its function is clearly stated in a memorandum of 1415: 'the turtle ship is capable of ramming the enemy fleet and causing damage to enemy vessels without incurring any itself'.

The introduction of the p'anokson

During their heyday the Japanese wako's favourite way of capturing a ship was by boarding party, and the usual style of Korean commercial ship, with a flat freeboard, unfortunately provided an ideal fighting ground for this. The first response was to build ships with simple raised gunwales behind which defenders could shelter. The Koreans then developed the *p'anokson* ('board-roofed' or 'superstructured' ships), which added an extra deck, so that the oarsmen below were separated from the fighting sailors above. A rudimentary castle on the deck provided a command post for the captain. The nearest equivalent to them in the Chinese typology was the *zhan xian*, or fighting junk (see Volume 1 of this work). Being typically Korean, the p'anokson was very solidly built, and the sizes of different p'anokson are usually noted as either 50, 60 or 70 feet long at the bottom plates, with the largest on record being 110 feet long. All had a complement of 125 men and had both sail and oar propulsion. They were often ornamented with dragons painted on the sides. Sturdy p'anokson such as these made up the vast majority of the ships in the Korean navy that fought the Japanese in 1592. At the battle of Okp'o, for example, we read of 25 p'anokson, 15 smaller fighting vessels and 46 other boats, probably civilian vessels requisitioned for the navy.

The turtle ship

The most famous Korean warship of all was the turtle ship, a vessel forever associated with the name of Admiral Yi Sun-sin, the saviour of

This illustration from the shrine to Admiral Yi at Noryang depicts the original type of turtle ship, based on the ramming turtle ship, of King T'aejong's reign in 1415. The dragon head is not overly large, and the bow is shown to be of very solid construction, ideal for the ramming role claimed for it. This version is referred to as the Tongjeyong type.

Korea. It is therefore strange that we have so little idea of what this celebrated battleship really looked like. The situation becomes more puzzling when one realises that after the time of Admiral Yi's triumphs the Korean navy went 'turtle ship mad', and there exists an impressive screen painting showing something that never existed during the 16th century: an entire fleet of turtle ships of different sizes, sporting dragon heads and with armoured shells. Long after the last surviving turtle ship had disintegrated in the mud of Inch'on harbour, the tradition lived on to such an extent that when Korea felt threatened by Western powers during the 19th century, owing to its treatment of foreign missionaries, the country's leading naval architect was commissioned to produce a fully armour-plated turtle ship 'just like the old days'. Even though the man feared for his head as much as his reputation, his creation stubbornly refused to float.

Back in the 16th century there was no confusion over either the turtle ship's form or its function. In terms of shape it lay full square in the long Korean tradition of ships that were both wide and solidly built. It was certainly strong enough to ram an enemy ship, but this was not its primary function. Nor was its enclosed structure any great innovation. The Chinese *meng chong* sported enclosed sidewalls and an open top deck, as did the existing Korean p'anokson. The turtle design, however, went one stage further than either of these by removing the castle from the deck of a p'anokson and roofing over the entire space. The resulting curved finish meant that the ship was completely enclosed. It certainly did resemble a turtle shell, and provided the man-made equivalent of its protection.

The customarily modest Admiral Yi Sun-sin would never have claimed to have been the inventor of the turtle ship, a role with which he is traditionally credited. Strictly speaking he revised an earlier style of the

The modifications and improvements Yi Sun-sin made to produce his new-style turtle ship resulted in the type known as the Chwasuyong ship. The new ship has six oars on each side rather than eight. The dragon head is now much more prominent, and another face has been added below. The higher sides show unmistakable gunports, and the hexagonal patterns on the curved roof make the whole vessel look much more like a sea turtle.

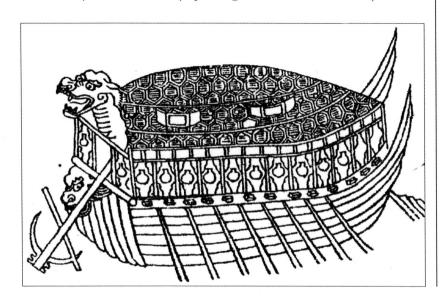

15th century, but his revival was very innovative. He first mentions the ship in his diary entries for the months leading up to the Japanese invasion of 1592. There are notes of the test firing of cannon from the deck of the turtle ship, and a reference to the purchase of material for its sails. The last test-firing session took place one day before the Japanese landed, but it is not until Yi's diary reports on the battle of Sach' on that we read of the deployment of his 'secret weapon'. 'Previously', writes Yi in his characteristic matter-of-fact style, 'I had had a turtle ship specially built.' There follows the longest description in all his writings of the vessel:

The turtle ship in the War Memorial Museum, Seoul, seen from above and showing the rows of spikes to discourage boarding. The flag bearing the character 'turtle' is also shown.

… with a dragon's head from whose mouth we could fire our cannons, and with iron spikes on its back to pierce the enemies' feet when they tried to board. Because it is in the shape of a turtle, our men can look out from inside, but the enemy cannot look in from outside. It moves so swiftly that it can plunge into the midst of even many hundreds of enemy vessels in any weather to attack them with cannon balls and fire throwers.

It is only Yi's nephew, writing after his uncle's tragic death at the last battle of the Korean War in 1598, who gives us any more detailed information:

Another special war vessel has been developed. About the size of a p'anokson its surface is planked, with narrow passageways through which sailors can move about. The whole surface of the ship, other than these passageways, is covered with spikes so that no enemy can walk over it. At the bow is a dragon head from which cannon can be fired; another cannon is installed at the stern. There are six gun ports on each side. It is called a turtle ship from its appearance. During battle, the spikes are hidden under straw mats as the ship charges into the enemy fleet.

So honoured was Yi after his death that his diary and his memorials to the Korean court were published in 1795 as *Yi Ch'ungmugong chonso* (the Collected Works of Admiral Yi). This work augments the above descriptions with dimensions of the turtle ship and the inclusion of two drawings, which unfortunately have tended to add to the confusion rather than reduce it. The first illustration probably depicts the

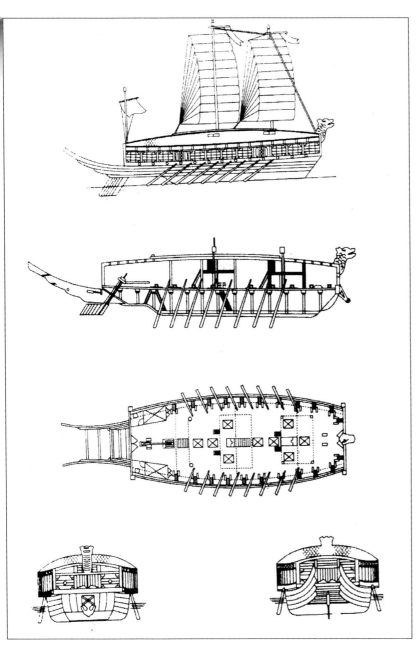

original turtle ship of King T'aejong's reign in 1415. The dragon head is not overly large, and the bow is shown to be of very solid construction, ideal for the ramming role claimed for it. This version is referred to as the Tongjeyong type. The second illustration shows a similar vessel but with some interesting modifications, and this has been identified as Yi's creation. The differences between the two pictures therefore represent the modifications and improvements Yi Sun-sin made to produce his new-style turtle ship, noted in the work as the Chwasuyong ship. The new ship has six oars on each side rather than eight. The dragon head is now much more prominent, and another face has been added below. The higher sides show unmistakable gunports, and the hexagonal patterns on the curved roof make the whole vessel look much more like a sea turtle.

It is from these two pictures that all modern attempts at reconstructing the turtle ship are derived, and models in museums within Korea and in other

Plan, end and side elevations of the turtle ship, based on the 1975 reconstruction drawings that have provided the basis for all reproductions since that date.

places from Beijing to Greenwich attest to the pitfalls of so doing. An early and worthy attempt was made by Horace Underwood, a missionary and scholar who loved Korea but who was no naval architect. Underwood's big problem, which he openly acknowledged, was where to put the oars, because the two drawings are somewhat ambiguous. His solution was to place them down in the lower part of the hull, which in real life would have led to all sorts of practical problems. This arrangement was published in his 1933 book *Korean Boats and Ships*, and led several museum re-creations up a blind alley, including those in the Hyonch'ungsa shrine in South Korea and the Central Historical Museum in P'yongyang. Nowadays the drawings are interpreted as indicating that the deck has an overhang from which the oars project downwards in the yuloh style. This would also give ample room for the fighting men, and retain the below-decks cabins which are a feature of the historical record. This modern interpretation of the Chwa-suyong drawing has been used as the template for every reconstruction made in recent times, such as the 1:5-scale turtle ship at Noryang on Namhae Island, the magnificent 1:2.5-scale ship inside the War Memorial Museum in Seoul, and the full-sized replica that lies at anchor at Yosu.

The armament of the turtle ship is described below, but the most intriguing feature concerns its turtle-like carapace. The accounts of Yi and his nephew confirm the presence of spikes, which are curiously missing from the 1795 drawings, but instead the Chwa-suyong ship has a pronounced hexagonal pattern on its 'shell'. The War Memorial Museum concluded that this was a representation of hexagonal armour plates from each of which a spike protruded. We noted in the previous volume that armour plating was not unknown on Chinese fighting ships, and Japanese sources mention the turtle ship being 'covered in iron'. There is also some fascinating circumstantial evidence from the Japanese side that strongly suggests that the turtle ships were firmly believed to be armour plated. Tokugawa Ieyasu, the future shogun of Japan, managed to avoid service in Korea, but was nonetheless expected to do his bit for the war effort. One way in which he exercised this was to respond to a request issued by Hideyoshi in 1593 to supply iron plates for use in building warships, so that the turtle ship could be countered on its own terms.

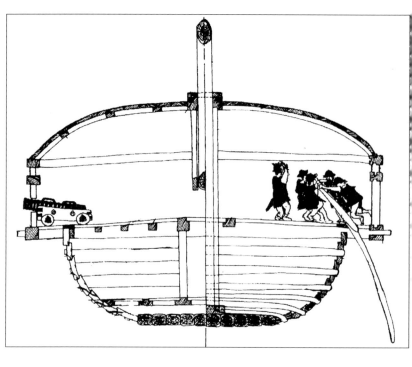

Cross-section of turtle ship with crewmen. The yuloh style of oar is clearly illustrated, and a 'heaven' cannon is rolled out for action.

KOREAN SHIPBOARD ARMAMENTS

Korean naval cannon

The Koreans always favoured bombardment in the Chinese style rather than use boarding parties, and the transmission of gunpowder technology from the Ming dynasty in 1373 is a pivotal event. The Koreans took rapidly to artillery, and ended up producing the most advanced range of shipboard cannon in East Asia, which they used against Japanese pirate ships in 1380 and 1383. By 1410, 160 Korean battleships are recorded as having artillery on board.

Mortars firing the Korean version of thunder-crash bombs, the hard-cased fragmentation projectiles of medieval China, are known to have

been used from ships' decks, but the favoured weapons were cannons mounted on mobile wooden carriages. There were four types of cannon in order of size: *chonja* (heaven), *chija* (earth), *hyonja* (black) and *hwangja* (yellow). The names have no particular significance and refer to the first four characters of a Chinese literary classic, thus making them effectively cannon types A, B, C and D. There

Korean 'black' and 'yellow' naval cannon in the War Memorial Museum, Seoul. The devastating wooden arrow tipped with iron lies at the weapon's side.

was also a smaller type of cannon used at sea that could be held resting on a bulwark and was called the *sungja* (victory), but it is important to note that the European-style arquebus, which had such an impact on Japan, did not appear in Korean warfare until the first siege of Chinju in 1593. Chinese cannon such as the 'great general' and 'crouching tiger' may also have been used at sea, but it is the above names that recur again and again.

The reinforced arrow

Stone and iron balls were fired from the Korean naval cannon, but the preferred projectiles were wooden arrows tipped with iron and with iron

or leather flights that made them look like rockets, although they were of course not self-propelled. The largest ones were nine feet long and were fired from the heaven-type cannons. They had a longer range and greater accuracy than cannon balls, but packed no less a punch when the iron head smashed into the side of a Japanese warship, sending deadly showers of wood splinters among the crew even if the ship was not holed through. They could also be very easily converted into fire arrows. Records of test firings held in Seoul noted the arrows burying themselves into the ground up to their iron 'feathers'.

A 'black' cannon on a reproduction naval carriage at the Chesungdang shrine on Hansando.

KOREAN FIGHTING SHIPS IN ACTION

The most detailed accounts of Korean fighting ships in action come from the war diaries and reports of Admiral Yi during the Korean War. The overall impression given is that the p'anokson's open upper deck was ideal for high-elevation shooting. It was effectively a battleship that bombarded the enemy from a distance.

In contrast, the technique for using a Korean turtle ship was the classic one for a vessel of this type: rapid advance as a vanguard vessel to break an enemy line, bombardment from a closer range than the open-decked p'anokson would allow, and speedy withdrawal, all of which may be found in the sometimes brief accounts of the turtle ship in action that appear in Yi's battle reports. It is variously described as 'shooting heaven, earth, black and yellow cannons' and 'darting against the enemy'. Less frequently we hear of it ramming its prey – this precious vessel was too valuable to risk damage from a collision. It is also important to note that there do not seem to have been more than five turtle ships in action at any one battle, and there was only one available during its first outing at Sach'on. The first naval battle of the Korean War took place at Okp'o off the eastern coast of Koje Island and involved only p'anokson. At the battle of Sach'on soon afterwards the turtle ship made its first appearance, to be followed by virtuoso performances at the battles of Tangp'o, Tanhangp'o and Yi's great victory at Hansando, where we read:

Then our ships suddenly enveloped the enemy craft from the four directions, attacking them from both flanks at full speed. The turtle with the Flying Squadron Chief on board rammed the enemy's pavilion vessel once again, while wrecking it with cannon fire, and our other ships hit its brocade curtains and sails with fire arrows. Furious flames burst out and the enemy commander fell dead from an arrow hit.

TECHNIQUES AND TYPES OF JAPANESE SHIPS AND SHIPBUILDING

The Japanese shipbuilding tradition

All Japanese writers trace the construction of early sea-going ships to continental Asia, and as the techniques of shipbuilding differed little from practices in China and Korea, it is unnecessary to go into great detail about Japanese ship construction except where it differs from continental practice. We see the identical use of the yuloh-type oar for example. There is also an interesting pictorial reference in a book called *Wakan Senyoshu* (Collection of Ships Used by the Japanese and Chinese) published in 1766. Two illustrations show ships being built using traditional techniques. In the first we see a flat keel being laid for what could be a *kobaya*-type of vessel (described below). The prow is acutely curved, and a carpenter is securing the planks using what appear to be metal clamps. A carpenter in the rear is using an adze. The second illustration resembles the description given above of a Korean ship being built, with the planks being added to make an open-ended box. The vessel seems to have reached the stage where the cross-members will be put in place.

Early Japanese fighting ships

Nothing is known of the precise type or design of ships that took Japanese troops to Korea and fought at the battle of the Paekch'on River during the 7th century, and it is only with the Gempei War of the 12th century that we start to get our first ideas of what a Japanese warship looked like. In fact the word 'warship' is something of a misnomer, because there is no evidence of the existence of any dedicated fighting-ship designs

A rare contemporary painting of a Japanese warship of the 14th century. It depicts a vessel of the early Muromachi Period, which dates from the establishment of the Ashikaga shogunate, so it is comparable with the ships that would have been used by the wako. A warship is clearly indicated, because it has soldiers on board, both samurai and footsoldiers. Note the deck castle and forecastle, both of which have white painted wooden sides, and the brocade curtains above the auxiliary oar power.

until the 16th century. Throughout the Heian and Kamakura Periods the vessels are 'ships used for fighting' rather than 'fighting ships'. There are no Chinese-style tower ships with multi-storey decks and trebuchets, just simple vessels crammed with samurai archers who have left their horses on the shore, and footsoldiers who have augmented their usual *naginata*, the polearm with a curved blade, with long rakes and hooked spears – yet even these were used in land warfare. The positive side is that we know quite a lot about the appearance of the ships and how they operated.

The most plentiful illustrative sources for 12th-century Japanese fighting ships are concerned with the naval battles of the Gempei War, particularly Dan no Ura in 1185. Although most were painted long after the event, there is a remarkable consistency in the way the ships are represented. First we have the large and ornate vessel that was the imperial flagship. It is propelled by oars and sails, and has a decorative one-storey superstructure surrounded by curtains similar to the *maku* used as a general's headquarters on a battlefield. During the battle of Dan no Ura the child emperor was transferred to one of the less ornate vessels, which saw much of the action. Their defences would be augmented by hanging curtains and placing wooden shields along the gunwales, the shields being the same types used by footsoldiers on the battlefield.

There are also many representations of smaller ships that resemble the simple Chinese patrol boats or even the sampan. They are propelled and steered by one oarsman in the stern using a yuloh-type oar, and are completely open with no defensive bulwarks. There is the occasional wooden shield, but no other protection for the handful of samurai who fight from them. They were therefore comparatively flimsy, and this may well account for the story of the Herculean archer Minamoto Tametomo sinking a ship with one arrow.

Almost identical vessels are found on the Mongol Invasion Scroll carrying the samurai on their 'little ship' raids of 1281, but larger boats were used also for this purpose, because we know that the mast of the Japanese ship was lowered to provide a gangplank for boarding. A very good reconstruction of one of these boats is found in the detailed illustration within this book.

Japanese pirate ships

The pirate ships of the 14th-century wako, of course, had to be sea-going vessels, and it is likely that they were just converted merchant junks, although Chinese paintings of wako raids also show the pirates operating from small boats. These are likely to have been seized from Koreans when they landed, or one may have been carried on the larger vessel to allow landing to take place while the pirate ship lay safely at anchor off shore. Details of 14th- and 15th-century ships are known to us from religious paintings of Buddhist priests who travelled abroad, and it is unlikely that the wako ships would have looked very different. They resemble Chinese sea-going junks in many particulars. As they had to carry the pirates to Korea and China, sail was the preferred means of propulsion, but auxiliary oars were also provided. There was an open deck with railings round it, and simple open wooden fighting castles at stem and stern. Larger versions had two masts and a central deck castle, and some illustrations show the popular Japanese feature of a cloth curtain hung round the gunwales.

Sengoku fighting ships: The ataka bune

With the Sengoku Period we begin to find clear accounts and descriptions of dedicated Japanese fighting ships for the first time. The warships operated by the daimyo of the Sengoku Period fell into the three categories of large, medium and small fighting ships. These are usually found under the names of *ataka bune*, *seki bune* and *kobaya*, but there are considerable overlaps between the three styles, some 'blended' versions and also a 'super-large' category.

The ataka bune was the battleship of any Sengoku daimyo's navy. It resembled the Korean p'anokson or the partially enclosed Chinese 'destroyers', but was much more solidly built and accordingly more sluggish, and looked like a floating wooden box. The whole of the side surface was one blank wall of thick wooden planks pierced with small loopholes for guns and bows protecting the oarsmen along with the samurai. There was an open upper deck protected by a low bulwark that was an extension of the sidewalls. In some versions a 'cabin', again very solidly built, sat on the deck. In addition to the oar propulsion there was a mast from which a large sail was hung bearing the daimyo's *mon* (badge) in a bold stencilled or painted design. The mast was pivoted centrally, and folded down when the ship went into action, and a door opened on to the flat-ended open bows where the anchors were stowed, while extra protection for the projecting oars could be given by hanging screens of bamboo outside them. The normal complement of an ataka bune was 80 oarsmen and 60 fighting men, with three cannon and 30 arquebuses. The importance of the standard

A Korean drawing of an extra large ataka bune of the Edo Period showing side, plan and elevation views. It is much sleeker than the earlier versions.

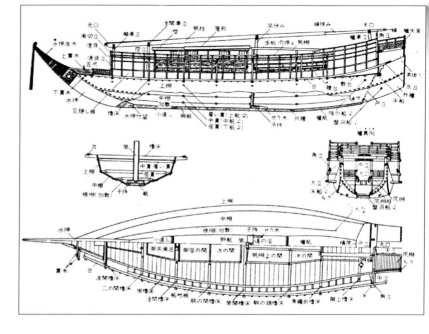

A: The Taira and Minamoto fight a 'land battle on the sea' at the battle of Mizushima, 1183

A

B: A gang of wako (Japanese pirates) disembark on the coast of Korea and begin a raid inland, 1380

B

C: Warships of the ataka bune and seki bune types are being used during the first battle of Kizugawaguchi between Oda Nobunaga and Mori Terumoto, 1576

C

D: The Korean turtle ship - pride of the Korean navy, 1592

D

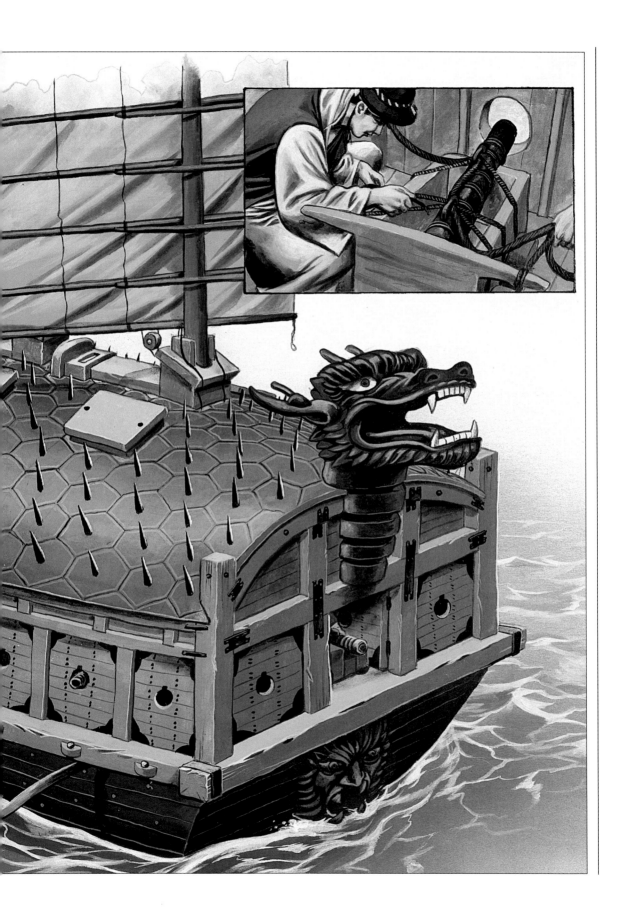

E: A Korean p'anokson ship lays down a fierce barrage of huge iron-tipped wooden arrows against the Japanese fleet at the battle of Okp'o, 1592

E

F: The *Nihon Maru*, flagship of the Japanese navy, is holed by a turtle ship during the battle of Angolp'o, 1592

F

G: A mekura bune, defended by bamboo palings, carries out a surprise ship-to-shore bombardment against an outlying fort of Osaka Castle, 1614 ataka bune as an all-purpose warship is illustrated by an order issued in 1609 by Tokugawa Ieyasu banning the daimyo from owning them. It is probably ataka bune that are being described at the battle of Tangp'o in Korea in 1592. There were 21 Japanese ships in all, and their formation was dominated by a large vessel with:

... a tall pavilion of about three body lengths, soaring high into the sky, surrounded by a red brocade curtain, painted on the outside and embroidered with a large yellow Chinese character on the four directions. Inside the pavilion was seen a Japanese Commander with a red parasol planted in front. He showed no expression of fear, like a man resigned to death.

Medium and small fighting ships: The seki bune and kobaya

The medium warship was known as a seki bune, which looked like a smaller version of the ataka bune but had a noticeably pointed bow tasselled with coiled rope. The protection was very similar but there was usually no deck house. The rudder was operated from the open deck. They were crewed by 40 oarsmen, and carried 30 fighting men armed with one cannon and 20 arquebuses. The seki bune formed the backbone of any feudal navy.

A seki bune, which looked like a smaller version of the ataka bune but had a noticeably pointed bow tasselled with coiled rope. The protection was very similar but there was usually no deck house. The rudder was operated from the open deck. They were crewed by 40 oarsmen, and carried 30 fighting men armed with one cannon and 20 arquebuses.

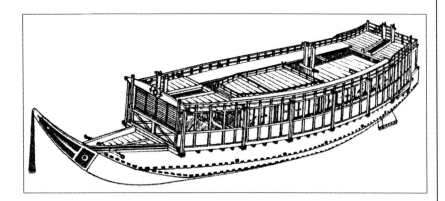

The *kobaya* was the smallest and fastest of the trio, and had no wooden planking as side protection, although some versions had wooden walls at the front. Instead an open wooden framework round the ship could have curtains hung from it, which would stop a spent arrow. Alternatively, bamboo walls or portable wooden shields like the ones used in the Gempei Wars could be added as a temporary measure. The kobaya had a crew of 20 oarsmen and carried ten fighting men and eight arquebuses. Some kobaya were the same size as a seki bune. All three types were used extensively during the Korean War.

The super-large fighting ships: O ataka bune

Another type of warship made its debut during the second of the two greatest naval battles on the domestic front during the Sengoku Period: the battles of Kizugawaguchi in 1576 and 1578. The name means 'the mouth of the Kizu River', because that is exactly where they were fought between Oda Nobunaga and Mori Terumoto. In 1576 Oda Nobunaga's admiral, Kuki Yoshitaka, attempted to set up a naval blockade against the Mori supply convoys sailing into the Kizu River and on to Ishiyama Honganji. The two fleets, both of which consisted of the three types noted above, met in battle, and Kuki's ships were heavily defeated. Two years later Oda Nobunaga tried again, and this time Kuki was in command of six specially commissioned large 'one-off' versions of the ataka bune. Known as *o ataka bune* (great ataka bune), they were huge, strong, had considerable firepower, and were totally unwieldy.

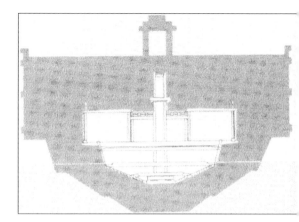

The accompanying illustration shows the size of an o ataka bune in comparison to the ordinary ataka bune, to which had been added an additional floor above the enclosed oarsmen's deck. Eyewitnesses described them as *tessen* (iron ships) – a phrase that has led to much unnecessary speculation as to whether they were yet another candidate for the title of the world's first ironclad battleship. They may well have been reinforced with iron plates – we have seen the technique used elsewhere – and it is a fact that they were very heavy. The flotilla of tessen was ambushed on its way from Ise Bay by some local pirates, but their cannon easily brushed off the attackers. When the battle of Kizugawaguchi began the Mori's arquebus bullets and cannon balls bounced off the sides of the iron ships, which is probably where any iron plating would have been added. Yet a major design fault was revealed when one was boarded, and the shift in weight to one side made it roll over and capsize.

A sketch showing the amazing difference in size between the ordinary ataka bune (shown inside) and Oda Nobunaga's 'one-off' tessen (iron ships). Known also as o ataka bune (great ataka bune).

The Japanese flagship: *Nihon maru*

On the whole, Japanese fighting ships do not appear to have possessed any individuality. There is, however, one notable exception: the Japanese warship known as *Nihon maru*, a name that is the equivalent of 'HMS Japan'. It was originally built by Kuki Yoshitaka in 1591 to be Toyotomi Hideyoshi's flagship, and the name reflected his ambition to go on from Japan to rule the world. It was very large in size, putting it in the tessen or o atake bune class, and the impressive superstructure, which made it look like a floating Japanese castle, contained three 18-mat rooms arranged in a three-storey 'keep' with white-washed walls under a graceful curved roof.

The site of the battle of Hansando, showing the modern lighthouse built in the shape of a turtle ship.

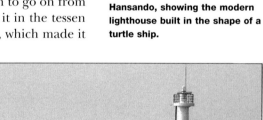

It was probably originally intended as a *goza bune* ('entertaining' ship), in other words Hideyoshi's 'royal yacht', and thus was designed to impress his visitors as much as his ornate palaces did, but during the Korean War it went into action during the battle of Angolp'o in 1592 under the command of Kuki Yoshitaka. Angolp'o came about as a result of the famous Japanese defeat by Admiral Yi's turtle ships at the battle of Hansando. The Japanese commander at Hansando, Wakizaka Yasuharu, had retired to the port of Angolp'o after the battle. Yi followed up his victory by attacking

The Japanese warship known as *Nihon maru*, a name that translates as 'HMS *Japan*'. It was originally built by Kuki Yoshitaka in 1591 to be Toyotomi Hideyoshi's flagship, and the name reflected his ambition to go on from Japan to rule the world. It was very large in size, putting it in the tessen or o ataka bune class, and its impressive superstructure made it look like a floating Japanese castle.

the Japanese fleet in Angolp'o harbour, and *Nihon maru* was in the thick of the action. The chronicle *Shima gunki* notes how *Nihon maru* was decorated with a 'Mount Horai', a Shinto decoration named after the sacred mountain of Chinese mythology, and that a brocade curtain, which had the practical function of stopping spent arrows, added to the decorative effect. The Koreans were clearly unimpressed by the religious augmentation of *Nihon maru*, and opened up on it with everything they possessed:

However, when the fire arrows came flying, we were ready and pulled the charred embers into the sea with ropes, and the ship was not touched. They fired as well from near at hand with half-bows [the short Korean composite bows], which went through the threefold curtain as far as the second fold, but ended up being stopped at the final layer. They then moved in at close range and when they fired the cannons they destroyed the central side of *Nihon maru* for three feet in each direction, but the carpenters had been ordered to prepare for this in advance, and promptly made repairs to keep out the sea water.

It is interesting to note that one Japanese account of the battle of Angolp'o also contains the only mention of turtle ships in the literature. They are referred to as being covered in iron and firing cannons, fire arrows and the large wooden rocket-like arrows.

Nihon maru survived the Korean War to see more service. When the campaign was over it was brought back to Toba where it was improved and refitted and renamed *Tairyu maru*. Here it remained until 1856 when it was so decayed that it was broken up. Its elaborate carved dragon figurehead was preserved at Ise for almost another century, but was destroyed during a US bombing raid in 1945.

Specialised Japanese fighting ships

The basic design of the Japanese warship, which, regardless of size, consisted of a rectangular wooden box above a hull, allowed several specialised variations from the trio of ataka bune, seki bune and kobaya. One was the *seiro bune*, or siege tower ship. It was adapted from a medium or large vessel, with a wooden siege tower of square cross section replacing the deckhouse. The tower was given stability by stout ropes that anchored its four top corners. Arquebusiers would be placed in the walled platform thus created at the top of the towers, and would fire down into a enemy castle from an advantageous height.

The *uma fune* or 'horse boat' was a specialised transport vessel designed for carrying horses. There are records of these ships being used by the Shimazu family during the Korean invasion. The horses were kept in the front part of the ship left open to the skies. The animals were winched aboard from the harbour side, supported under the belly by a sling, using a rope and a pulley attached to the top of the mast.

During the Osaka campaign of 1614–15 another form of specialised warship made its appearance in Japan. This was the *mekura bune* (literally 'blind ship'), very similar to a kobaya, but instead of the cloth curtains that were hung from the kobaya's surrounding frame, one-foot-diameter bamboo bundles were suspended to give a light but absorbent protective screen all round. A pitched bamboo roof of similar construction lay along the boat. Four square holes were cut on each side, through which poked the barrels of eight European breech-loading swivel guns with their mounting spikes sunk into the vertical posts of the mekura bune's sides. Each gun had a crew of three men: a loader, who dropped the breech container into the space and forced a retaining wedge in behind it; the aimer, whose hands were on the wooden tiller added behind the breech; and the firer, who stood ready with a fuse on a short linstock. To make room for these eight guns and their crews the number of oars was cut back to 18 on each side. Mekura bune were used in rapid journeys up and down the waterways around Osaka, firing the Japanese equivalent of a broadside into the walls of the outlying forts of the Osaka complex.

A Korean 'yellow' cannon mounted on a swivel into a wooden naval carriage. This was the smallest of the four types of cannon used in the Korean War against the Japanese.

JAPANESE SHIPBOARD ARMAMENTS

Fighting ships and crossbows

The first recorded instance of Japanese troops being involved in naval warfare is the battle of the Paekch'on River in Korea in 663, although details are lacking. The battle began when the Japanese fleet engaged the Tang fleet of 170 ships on the river and then withdrew, but we are not told how they fought. The account continues as follows:

So they again led forward the routed Japanese ranks, and troops of the middle division with their force, to attack the Great Tang fleet. But Tang closed upon them from right and left, and engaged them from all sides. In a short space of time, the imperial [Japanese] force was defeated, and many fell into the water and drowned. The ships were unable to manoeuvre either astern or ahead.

The last sentence implies a naval melee where the main means of fighting were grappling and boarding helped by crossbow fire, and it was to be Japanese crossbow fire that turned the tide in favour of the Japanese when they defeated a Silla fleet off Tsushima in 894. One hundred Silla ships with 2,500 men on board sailed into battle and were beaten when the governor of Tsushima 'raised shields and arranged crossbows'.

The fighting ship as a floating battlefield

By the time of the Gempei War of 1180–85 the crossbow was almost forgotten except as a siege weapon, and the longbow reigned supreme in the three instances of naval warfare that have come down to us from this epic conflict. The first was the battle of Mizushima in 1183, which provides the classic example of Japanese warriors having no consideration for naval tactics, and fighting as if the ships were merely an extension of dry land. At Mizushima the analogy is greatly strengthened when one reads that, 'the Taira ships were made fast alongside each other by hawsers from the stem and stern, and between these hawsers other ropes were fastened, on which planks were stretched for walking, so that the whole fleet became like a level surface for the fighting men.'

The description of the fighting that follows therefore sounds very much like a land battle, with an exchange of arrows and single combat, the only difference being that both grapplers and wounded fell into the sea. However, one of the Minamoto samurai, Yada Yoshikiyo, then 'sprang into a small boat with six of his retainers, and led a fierce attack in the very forefront of the battle, but all in vain, for his boat was capsized by the enemy and all in it were drowned'.

Admiral Yi's ally Chen Lin of Ming China fights the Japanese from junk-like ships with elaborate bows.

After the battle of Ichi no tani in 1184 the Taira escaped by sea because the Minamoto lacked the means to pursue them, and there was no more sea fighting until the battle of Yashima. Here there was no artificial platform, but still the same emphasis on archery warfare and single combat. On one occasion Minamoto Yoshitsune was chased from ship to ship by his would-be captors, and elsewhere he risked his life to retrieve his bow from the water, because it was so small compared to the bow of his famous uncle Tametomo, and he did not want to be ridiculed by the Taira. The battle of Yashima then continued on land. By the time of the most decisive battle of the Gempei Wars, the sea battle at Dan no Ura in 1185, both sides possessed fleets, and the tactical use made of them shows that true naval warfare had finally arrived in Japan.

Hand-held gunpowder weapons and boarding parties

The predatory, prize-seeking piratical world of the wako naturally espoused boarding techniques. There was nothing to be gained by sinking one's prey, yet even in the mainstream situation throughout Japanese history the attitude towards naval warfare remains remarkably consistent, and the only real change that we note during the Sengoku Period consequent on the introduction of firearms is the gradual replacement of the bow and arrow by the arquebus and bullet. Yet the principle remained exactly the same: sweep the enemy decks with missile fire and then engage in hand-to-hand fighting. These were the tactics adopted at the two battles of Kizugawaguchi. In the end it was probably the effect of the greatest samurai tradition of all, that of seeking out a worthy opponent and fighting him in single combat with a samurai sword, that led to such a technique dominating naval warfare as much as it did the battlefield. It may often have been only an ideal, but it was an ideal in which everyone believed.

The naval battles of the Korean War again show the same emphasis on boarding – not that Admiral Yi allowed this to happen very often, because his policy of bombardment meant that few Japanese ships ever managed to get close enough. At the battle of Ungch'on in 1593 Wakizaka Yasuharu and Kato Yoshiaki managed to lodge grappling hooks on to the same Korean warship at the same time. The angry Wakizaka ordered his men to cut Kato's grappling ropes, and while they were squabbling the Korean ship got away. Yi's diary also notes seeing at the battle of Myongyang in 1597, 'the enemy hoards like black ants climbing up An Wi's ship, but using sharp-edged clubs, long spears and sea-washed stones, the boarders were repelled.'

In fact it was only during the battle of Ch'ilch'onnyang against the useless Admiral Won Kyun that these Japanese tactics worked. To the sound of drums and gongs, and under a hail of fire arrows, the samurai boarded and took many heads.

The battle of Sunch'on, which took place almost at the end of the Korean War, involved boarding parties, but in a bizarre and farcical situation. It was the agreed role of the Ming naval commander Chen Lin that his ships should sail up to Sunch'on castle with the incoming tide and bombard its walls ready for a land assault. Unfortunately for the Chinese, the tide turned and left many ships stranded, which the Japanese interpreted as a deliberate attempt at an amphibious landing. The garrison samurai climbed on board the stricken vessels, and captured five of them, destroying 12 more.

This illustration details the use of rakes from a Japanese ship at the battle of Dan no Ura in 1185, whilst also showing shields with the mon of the Taira upon them.

The Japanese fondness for the use of boarding parties led to the creation of some interesting grappling irons. The *kusari kagi* was a device consisting of four hooks cold-welded together to which a short length of chain was attached. The other end of the chain was fixed to a stout pole. The *kama*, which had a sickle-like blade on the end of a ten-feet-long pole was used to counter the kusari kagi by cutting through the shaft. The *kumade* (bear paw) and the *kumode* (spiked bear paw) were also used for gaining a purchase on an enemy vessel, but also proved to be useful anti-personnel weapons.

Shipboard artillery and ship-to-shore bombardment

Descriptions of the use of shipboard bombardment from Japanese vessels is rather more difficult to find than those of boarding parties, and the most prominent references to it are found not in accounts of naval battles but in descriptions of sieges, with vessels providing ship-to-shore fire. The first example of naval bombardment in Japanese history is the siege of Moji castle in 1561, but there the naval bombardment was provided by Portuguese ships whose captains were taking an immense political risk. Some heavy-calibre pieces (probably breech loaders) were used in 1584 at Okita Nawate to support a column moving along a beach, with the gunners saying their prayers as they loaded, but there are almost no examples of anything heavier because of the absence of true naval cannon in Japan until comparatively late in samurai history. When European ships docked in Japanese ports, particularly from the time of the battle of Sekigahara onwards, their cannon would be more valued as a commodity than the goods they were carrying. However, any such cannon acquired in this way were not then remounted on to Japanese ships but used as siege weapons. The ataka bune clearly could not have stood the strain of a contemporary European culverin.

As a result, when we read that at the sieges of the Ikko-ikki fortress of Nagashima in 1573 and 1574 Oda Nobunaga's fleet bombarded the sectarians, we may best infer large-calibre arquebuses rather than European-style ships' cannons. Also, when Admiral Yi bewailed the loss of some Korean 'heaven' and 'black' cannons to the Japanese, he was referring to them being mounted on shore batteries, not Japanese ships, and it is not until the naval actions against Osaka in 1614 that we can identify true ship-to-shore bombardment.

As for the use of shore batteries to repulse ships, the year 1633 saw the most bizarre example of coastal naval warfare in Asian history. When the Japanese

The gunports on the turtle ship at Noryang. Note also the simple iron reinforcements, which may have given rise to the claims that the turtle ship was an ironclad battleship.

adventurer Yamada Nagamasa was murdered in Siam in 1633, an attack was launched on the Japanese settlement, and eight of Yamada's samurai were put in jail. Meanwhile some 'Java people', a vague expression that may indicate Vietnamese or Cambodian pirates in war barges, took the opportunity of the confusion to raid Siam. The Siamese king, realising that the Japanese 'belonged to a nation more feared by the Southerners than a fierce tiger', promised the eight prisoners their liberty if they would help rid his country of the invaders. The Japanese acted with alacrity, and proposed that as many Siamese as possible should be equipped with Japanese armour and helmets because the sight of a large Japanese army would terrify the attackers, and that eight elephants should also be made available. Seventy suits of Japanese armour were found, and an equal number of Siamese were dressed up in them. The eight samurai took command of 500 Siamese soldiers in all, and placed a couple of small cannon on the howdah of each elephant. 'As soon as they came in sight of the Java ships, they began a furious cannonade,' wrote the chronicler, 'which would speedily have sunk the whole fleet, had they not prudently retreated.' Thus did Japanese samurai disperse a Southeast Asian pirate fleet by a shore battery mounted on elephants.

Fire arrows and firebombs

Fire arrows shot from ordinary bows, and larger varieties like the Korean wooden arrows fired from cannon, were also used on board Japanese fighting ships during the Sengoku Period. Spherical bombs called *horokubiya* (cooking-pot fire arrows) and incendiaries were often

Diagram of Japanese naval battle formations: 1. The normal formation for advancing. 2. Tsuruyoku: a concave attack formation with wings advanced. 3. Hoen: a secure formation whereby the subsidiary vessels formed a complete circle round the flagship. 4. Ganko: the subsidiary vessels sail at an angle to the line of advance. 5. Gyorin: a defensive arrangement with all the subsidiary ships forward.

used in ship-to-ship combat. Sakuma Uemon, one of Oda Nobunaga's generals, had his ship set on fire by one thrown by the Mori. On the whole these bombs resembled the Chinese models in their construction, being of iron, ceramic material or layers of paper. One was swung round the head on a rope and then released. Others could be flung by a net on a pole rather like a game of lacrosse, or launched from traction trebuchets.

JAPANESE FIGHTING SHIPS IN ACTION

Naval tactics and battle formations

When a Japanese fleet of the Sengoku Period sailed into battle it was customary for the commander in chief to occupy a central position in the formation, much as he would have done on land. The main body would consist of ataka bune and seki bune, with kobaya acting in a communications role. Just as in land warfare, there existed a series of standard naval formations to cover different situations, all of which had similar names to the battle formations on land. The normal formation was for the flagship to be screened towards the front and sides by its support vessels. *Tsuruyoku* (crane's wing) was a concave attack formation with wings advanced. *Hoen* was a secure formation whereby the subsidiary vessels formed a complete circle round the flagship. In *ganko* the subsidiary vessels sailed at an angle to the line of advance. *Gyorin* was a defensive arrangement with all the subsidiary ships forward, and could easily be converted into an aggressive formation.

The battle of Dan no Ura in 1185, showing the full range of contemporary Japanese fighting ships described in the text.

The battle of Dan no Ura, 1185

The battle of Dan no Ura, which brought the Gempei War to an end in 1185, is Japan's most famous sea battle, and, as one of the most decisive battles in Japanese history, provides an interesting case study. The Minamoto ships went into battle with bows and sterns abreast while the Taira formed three squadrons, and a long-range archery duel began. The Taira took the initiative in the early stages because the tide conditions were in their favour, and Taira Tomomori, who was a good seaman, used his experience and knowledge of the tidal conditions in the strait. At the start of the battle there was an ebb tide flowing slowly into the Inland Sea, so the Taira ships attempted to surround the Minamoto fleet. By 11.00 a.m. the two fleets were closely engaged with sword and dagger fighting, but at about this time the tide changed and began to flow westwards out of the strait. This gave the advantage to the Minamoto, who exploited it to the full. Gradually the battle turned in their favour, and victory was assured when one of the Taira commanders, Miura Yoshizumi, turned traitor and attacked the Taira from

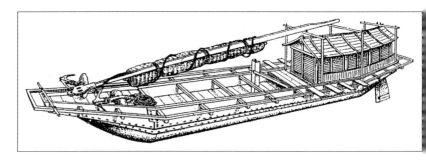

A Japanese ship of the Mongol invasion time. These were the larger variety of the ships that took part in the 'little ships' raids on the Mongol fleet.

the rear. He was also able to inform the Minamoto that the largest ship in the fleet did not contain the emperor, so the Minamoto turned their forces on to the correct target. The Minamoto archers first concentrated their fire on the rowers and the helmsmen, so that the Taira ships were soon out of control, and began to drift back with the tide. Realising that the battle was lost, many of the Taira committed suicide by jumping into the sea, and the child emperor Antoku was deliberately drowned to save him from capture.

Japanese fighting ships and combined operations

So strong was the Japanese tradition of the noble samurai seeking out a worthy opponent that there are several instances in Japanese history of an army and a navy co-operating to launch a combined operation. We conclude this work with two examples, the first being the use of small fighting ships against the Mongols.

The famous 'little ship' raids of the second Mongol invasion in 1281 lies full square within the samurai tradition, as we see illustrated in various sections of the Mongol Invasion Scroll. A Japanese boat, holding between ten and 15 samurai, would close with a Mongol ship under cover of darkness and lower its own mast to make a bridge for boarding. The samurai would then engage in hand-to-hand fighting with their swords. On one occasion 30 samurai even swam out to a Mongol ship, decapitated the entire crew, and then swam back. A certain Kusano Jiro led a raid in broad daylight and set fire to a ship even though his left arm was cut off. Kono Michiari also led a daytime raid with two boats. Thinking the Japanese were coming to surrender, the

A print of the battle of Miyajima in 1555, showing the Mori fleet sailing through the great torii (Shinto gateway) that marks the entrance to the shrine.

Mongols allowed them to come close, at which point they were boarded and a high-ranking general was captured. The Mongol response to the raids was to stretch chains between their ships so that the boats could not come close. Stones were also launched from traction trebuchets to sink the Japanese vessels.

These raids were so successful that the northern Mongol fleet was forced to

withdraw to Iki Island, there to await the arrival of the southern Chinese contingent. They eventually made rendezvous near the island of Takashima, where the Japanese launched a bold assault. The fighting lasted a full day and night, but the Japanese were eventually driven off by sheer weight of numbers. It was then that the kami kaze blew, and completed their work for them.

The battle of Miyajima, 1555

The Mori family of Hiroshima had a long naval tradition, and took great pride in their fleet, without which they could not have pulled off the most famous amphibious expedition in samurai history when Mori Motonari defeated Sue Harukata on the holy island of Miyajima in 1555. Sue had overthrown their former daimyo Ouchi Yoshitaka, whose demise gave Mori Motonari the perfect excuse to avenge his late lord and take his territories from the former comrade who had done the dirty work. Mori Motonari's officers suggested fortifying the island of Miyajima, also known as Itsukushima, which lies about a mile from the mainland. Mori felt that it would be an unwise move because an enemy could then isolate whoever was based there. However, he then decided to trick Sue Harukata into occupying Miyajima. As Mori controlled much of the seas around, it was then a simple task for him to launch an amphibious operation and destroy Sue's army. Under cover of a dark night and a blinding rainstorm Mori Motonari and his two sons, Mori Takamoto and Kikkawa Motoharu, sailed secretly round the northern tip of the island. Meanwhile Mori's other son, Kobayakawa Takakage, sailed up the strait in full view of Sue's lookouts, but then doubled back and made a frontal assault at dawn, synchronised with an advance by the other Mori from the rear.

SUGGESTIONS FOR FURTHER READING

Bonar, H.C., 'On Maritime Enterprise in Japan', reprinted in Stephen Turnbull (ed) *The Samurai Tradition* (Japan Library, 2000)

Sang-won Jeon, *Science and Technology in Korea: Traditional Instruments and Techniques* (Cambridge, Massachusetts: MIT Press, 1974)

Needham, Joseph, *Science and Civilisation in China, Volume 4: Physics and Physical Technology Part III: Civil Engineering and Nautics* (Cambridge: Cambridge University Press, 1971)

Purvis, F.P., 'Ship construction in Japan', in *Transactions of the Asiatic Society of Japan* Volume 47 (1919) pp1–22

Turnbull, Stephen, *Samurai Warfare* (Cassell, 1996)

Turnbull, Stephen, *Siege Weapons of the Far East*, Volume 1 (Osprey New Vanguard Series, 2001)

Turnbull, Stephen, *Siege Weapons of the Far East*, Volume 2 (Osprey New Vanguard Series, 2002)

Turnbull, Stephen, *Samurai Invasion: Japan's Korean War 1592–98* (Cassell, 2002)

Underwood, Horace, *Korean Boats and Ships* (Yonseu University Press, Seoul reprint 1979)

COLOUR PLATE COMMENTARY

A: THE TAIRA AND MINAMOTO FIGHT A 'LAND BATTLE ON THE SEA' AT THE BATTLE OF MIZUSHIMA, 1183

The battle of Mizushima in 1183 provides the classic example of Japanese warriors having no consideration for naval tactics, and fighting as if the ships were merely an extension of dry land. At Mizushima the analogy is greatly strengthened when one reads that 'the Taira ships were made fast alongside each other by hawsers from the stem and stern, and between these hawsers other ropes were fastened, on which planks were stretched for walking, so that the whole fleet became like a level surface for the fighting men.' The description of the fighting that follows therefore sounds very much like a land battle, with an exchange of arrows and single combat, the only difference being that both grapplers and wounded fell into the sea.

In this plate an attempt has been made to reconstruct this unusual struggle. The boats that have been fastened together were probably quite simple ones, and are based on contemporary designs. The ornate flagship floating behind them follows descriptions of the largest size of ship used during the Gempei War. There is also a great deal of archery taking place.

B: A GANG OF WAKO (JAPANESE PIRATES) DISEMBARK ON THE COAST OF KOREA AND BEGIN A RAID INLAND, 1380

In the 14th century the confusion caused by the Nanbokucho Wars between rival emperors of Japan provided the opportunity for the wako (pirates) to flourish, and during the ten years between 1376 and 1385 there were 174 recorded raids on Korea. Some of these expeditions amounted to short-term invasions of Korea, with as many as 3,000 penetrating far from the coast. In this plate, which is based on a contemporary Chinese scroll, we see the wako landing on the

The site of the battle of Miyajima in 1555, the shrine of Itsukushima, which appears to float on the water when the tide is in.

Korean coasts to begin their ravages. They are quite simply dressed, with little in the way of armour, but with very fierce-looking Japanese swords and spears.

The pirate ships had to be sea-going vessels, and it is likely that they were just converted merchant junks, although Chinese paintings of wako raids also show them operating from small boats. Details of 14th- and 15th-century ships are known to us from religious paintings of Buddhist priests who travelled abroad, and it is unlikely that the wako ships would have looked very different. They resemble Chinese sea-going junks in many particulars. As they had to carry the pirates to Korea and China, sail was the preferred means of propulsion, but auxiliary oars were also provided. There was an open deck with railings round it, and simple open wooden fighting castles at stem and stern. Larger versions had two masts and a central deck castle, and some illustrations show the popular Japanese feature of a cloth curtain hung round the gunwales.

C: WARSHIPS OF THE ATAKA BUNE AND SEKI BUNE TYPES ARE USED DURING THE FIRST BATTLE OF KIZUGAWAGUCHI BETWEEN ODA NOBUNAGA AND MORI TERUMOTO, 1576

The ataka bune was the battleship of any Sengoku daimyo's navy. It was solidly built but quite sluggish, and looked like a floating wooden box. The whole of the side surface was one blank wall of thick wooden planks pierced with small loopholes for guns and bows, protecting the oarsmen along with the samurai. There was an open upper deck protected by a low bulwark that was an extension of the sidewalls. In some versions a 'cabin', again very solidly

A model of an ataka bune ship used by the Takeda. Note the Takeda mon on the sail, which looks insufficient to move the clumsy vessel. The ataka bune was the battleship of a Sengoku daimyos' navy. It resembled the Korean p'anokson or the partially enclosed Chinese 'destroyers', but was much more solidly built and accordingly more sluggish, and looked like a floating wooden box. The whole of the side surface was one blank wall of thick wooden planks pierced with small loopholes for guns and bows, protecting the oarsmen along with the samurai.

built, sat on the deck. In addition to oar propulsion there was a mast from which a large sail was hung bearing the daimyo's mon (badge) in a bold stencilled or painted design. The mast was pivoted centrally, and folded down when the ship went into action, and a door opened on to the flat-ended open bows where the anchors were stowed. The medium warship was known as a seki bune, which looked like a smaller version of the ataka bune but had a noticeably pointed bow tasselled with coiled rope. The protection was very similar but there was usually no deck house. The rudder was operated from the open deck. They were crewed by 40 oarsmen, and carried 30 fighting men armed with one cannon and 20 arquebuses. The seki bune formed the backbone of any feudal navy.At the rear we have included one version of the kobaya, the lightest of the three standard fighting ships. This one has lower side rails than the kobaya shown on page 47. The kobaya was more manoeuvrable than a seki bune, even though many were of a similar size.

D: THE KOREAN TURTLE SHIP - PRIDE OF THE KOREAN NAVY, 1592

The most famous Korean warship of all was the turtle ship, a vessel forever associated with Admiral Yi Sun-sin, the saviour of Korea. In terms of shape it lay full square in the long Korean tradition of ships that were both wide and solidly built. It was certainly strong enough to ram an enemy ship, but this was not its primary function. The resulting curved finish of the roof meant that the ship was completely enclosed. It certainly did resemble a turtle shell, and provided the man-made equivalent of its protection. The ship had six oars on each side. The dragon head was prominent, and another face was added below. The high sides show unmistakable gunports, and the hexagonal patterns on the curved roof make the whole vessel look much like a sea turtle.

The reconstruction here is based on the reproduction turtle ship in the War Memorial Museum, Seoul, and the 1:1 vessel at Yosu. It has a shell of hexagonal metal plates with central spikes, and is built very solidly from stout timbers in typical Korean style. The sail is shown in use to illustrate its construction. There is a cannon underneath the ornate figurehead, and others down the side. The cutaway section shows a team of oarsmen operating a typical yuloh-type oar, which is screwed through the water rather than being dragged. Beind them, a cannon is being rolled out for action. This is shown in greater detail in the inset diagram at top right, which shows how the cannon barrel was secured by ropes to the simple box-like gun carriage.

E: A KOREAN P'ANOKSON SHIP LAYS DOWN A FIERCE BARRAGE OF HUGE IRON-TIPPED WOODEN ARROWS AGAINST THE JAPANESE FLEET AT THE BATTLE OF OKP'O, 1592

Here we see the main vessel type of the Korean navy blasting the Japanese fleet during the first naval encounter of the Korean War. The p'anokson ('board-roofed' or 'superstructured' ships) had two decks, so that the oarsmen below were separated from the fighting sailors above. A rudimentary castle on the deck provided a command post for the captain. Being typically Korean, the p'anokson was very solidly built, and the sizes of different p'anokson are usually noted as being either 50, 60 or 70 feet long at the bottom plates, with the largest on record being 110 feet long. All had a complement of 125 men and had both sail and oar propulsion. They were often ornamented with dragons painted on the sides. Sturdy p'anokson such as these made up the vast majority of the ships in the Korean navy that fought the Japanese in 1592. At the battle of Okp'o, for example, we read of 25 p'anokson.

The Koreans always favoured bombardment in the Chinese style rather than boarding, and ended up producing the most advanced range of shipboard cannon in East Asia. Here we see their favoured weapon; cannon mounted on mobile wooden carriages. Admiral Yi directs action from the deck castle. Contrary to popular belief, Admiral Yi never commanded a turtle ship in battle. In addition to cannon, bows are used. The inset diagram shows a cross-section.

A painting from the Hyonch'ungsa shrine, a memorial to Admiral Yi, showing Yi inspecting plans for the turtle ship. In the background the first turtle ship of Yi's design is taking shape.

F: THE *NIHON MARU*, FLAGSHIP OF THE JAPANESE NAVY, IS HOLED BY A TURTLE SHIP DURING THE BATTLE OF ANGOLP'O, 1592

Nihon maru, a name that translates as 'HMS *Japan*', was originally built by Kuki Yoshitaka in 1591 to be Toyotomi Hideyoshi's flagship, and the name reflected his ambition to go on from Japan to rule the world. It was very large in size, putting it in the tessen or o atake bune class, and the impressive superstructure, which made it look like a floating Japanese castle, contained three 18-mat rooms arranged in a three-storey 'keep' with white-washed walls under a graceful curved roof. It was probably originally intended as Hideyoshi's royal yacht, and thus designed to impress his visitors as much as his ornate palaces did, but during the Korean War it went into action during the battle of Angolp'o in 1592 under the command of Kuki Yoshitaka.

Angolp'o came about as a result of the famous Japanese defeat by Admiral Yi's turtle ships at the battle of Hansando. The Koreans fired conventional bows and arrows, which went through the threefold curtain as far as the second fold, but ended up being stopped at the final layer. They then moved in at close range, and when they fired the cannons they destroyed the central side of *Nihon maru* for three feet in each direction, but the carpenters had been ordered to prepare for this in advance, and promptly made repairs. The moment of impact by Korean cannonballs is shown. Splinters fly in all directions. Note how the turtleship has packed away its sails before going into action.

G: A MEKURA BUNE, DEFENDED BY BAMBOO PALINGS, CARRIES OUT A SURPRISE SHIP-TO-SHORE BOMBARDMENT AGAINST AN OUTLYING FORT OF OSAKA CASTLE, 1614

The mekura bune (literally 'blind ship') was very similar to a kobaya, the smallest and fastest of the standard Japanese ships, which had no wooden planking as side protection, although some versions had wooden walls at the front. Instead of the cloth curtains that were hung from the kobaya's surrounding frame, one-foot-diameter bamboo bundles were suspended to give a light but absorbent protective screen all round. A pitched bamboo roof of similar construction lay along the boat. Four square holes were cut on each side, through which poked the barrels of eight European breech-loading swivel guns with their mounting spikes sunk into the vertical posts of the mekura bune's sides. Each gun had a crew of three men: a loader who dropped the breech container into the space and forced a retaining wedge in behind it; the aimer, whose hands were on the wooden tiller added behind the breech; and the firer, who stood ready with a fuse on a short linstock. To make room for these eight guns and their crews the number of oars was cut back to 18 on each side.

The wooden walls of the Osaka forts were particularly susceptible to bombardment from cannonballs. The mekura bune carries flags bearing the Tokugawa mon (badge). In the first inset diagram, the three-man crew are shown in action. The breech-tube is being lowered into the rear of the muzzle. The central diagram shows the protection afforded In the bows of the vessel by a hinged door. To the right we see a cross-section showing the oarsmen and gunners. There is a heavy layer of ballast around the heel.

The 1:2.5-scale reproduction turtle ship in the War Memorial Museum, Seoul. This is regarded as the most accurate representation of this famous vessel, showing the two figureheads and the auxiliary sails.

The kobaya had no wooden planking as side protection, although some versions had wooden walls at the front. Instead an open wooden framework round the ship could have curtains hung from it, which would stop a spent arrow. Alternatively, bamboo walls or portable wooden shields like the ones used in the Gempei Wars could be added as a temporary measure. The kobaya had a crew of 20 oarsmen and carried ten fighting men and eight arquebuses.

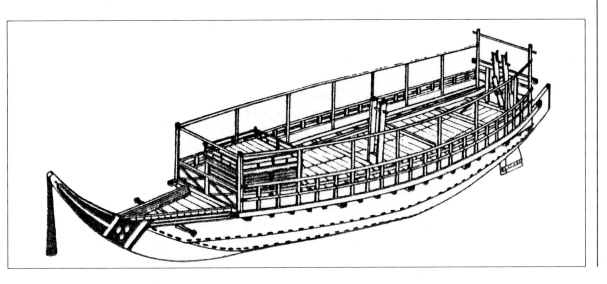

INDEX